elements of an adored mind
by shannon ellis

elements of an adored mind

Copyright © 2019 by Shannon Ellis
All rights reserved. No part of this publication may be reproduced, distributed, or transmitted in any form or by any means, including photocopying, recording, or other electronic or mechanical methods, without the prior written permission of the publisher, except in the case of brief quotations embodied in critical reviews and certain other noncommercial uses permitted by copyright law.

First Printing, 2019
Printing information available on the last page.

ISBN 978-1-9992272-4-1 (sc)
ISBN 978-1-9992272-5-8 (e)

Editor: Ava Balis
Illustrator: Ruben Ramires
Riza Publishing Press
Ottawa, ON, Canada
www.rizapress.com

illustrated by
ruben ramires

a dedication:
To Christine, you were a light in many people's lives and always helped me to carry on pursuing my dream. In part, this book is due to people like you. You loved fiercely and selflessly, you were an incredible mother to my best friend and now I'll look for your light among the stars. Rest beautifully x

table of contents

the sunshine

soleil 9
curly headed lovers 10
the first hello 11
quiet nights 13
bare connections 14
love 15

the wind

quarantined 19
secrets 22
close encounters 24
underground 26
concrete 27
dodgy conversations at a bus stop 28

the clouds

the last summer 31
readjustment 32
bittersweet 33
gold dust 34
cherry wine 36
embers 37
sipping tea 38

the rain

daisy plucker 43
distance 45
podcast 47
remnants 48
acquainted strangers 50
heart 51
exhibition 52
passive transport mind strings 53

the thunderstorm

trigger run 57
father 58
soap 60
manner 61
harsh 63

the rainbow

familiar 67
ode to my bedsheets 68
buttons 69
acquired astrology 70
chords 72
fault lines 73
your daughter 75

the sunshine

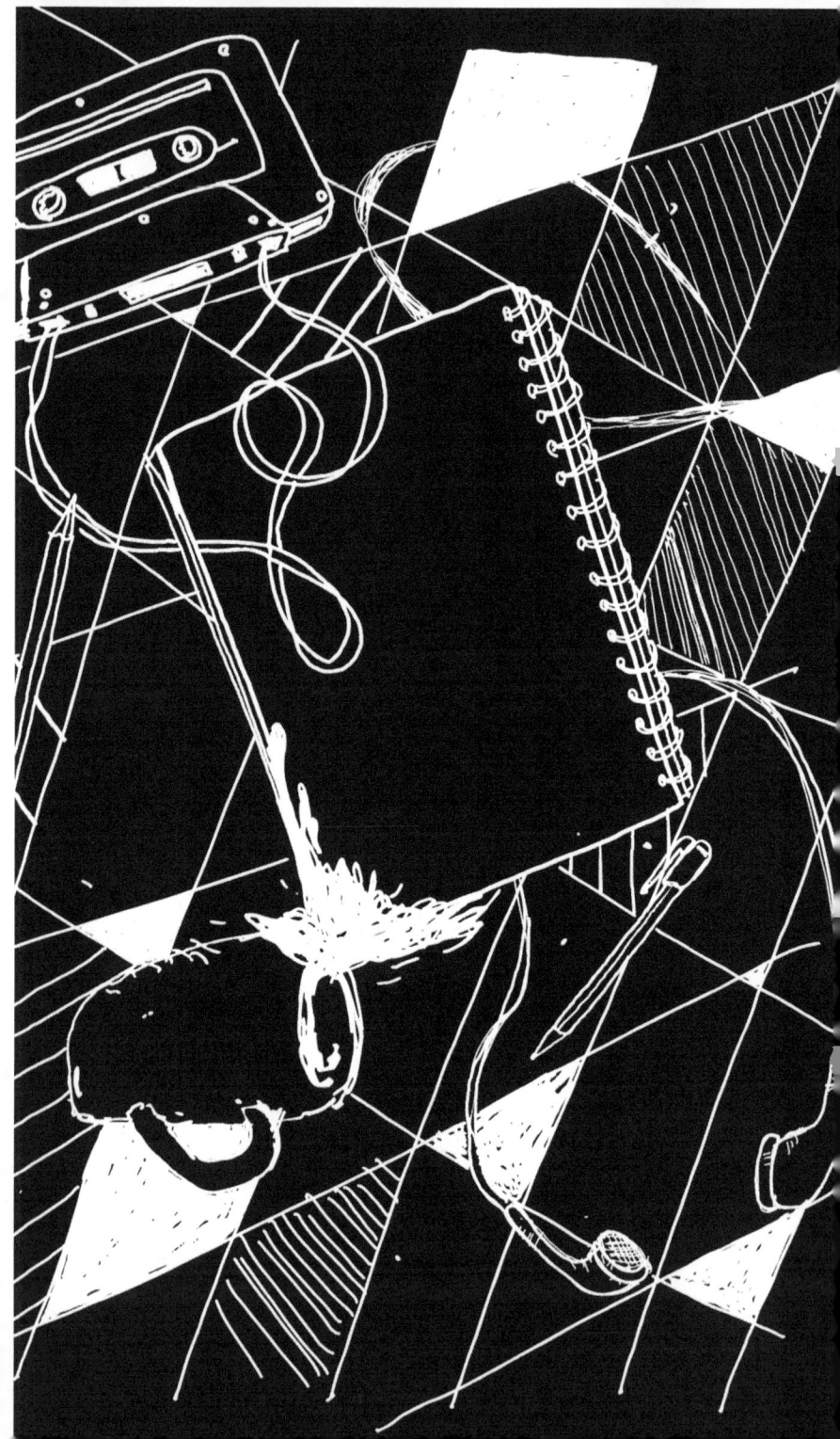

elements of an adored mind

soleil

early morning sunrise
that warm light coming in to land
on the runway of my eyes.

it welcomes me with a rattled thud and disperses slowly
into the gravel of my tired aching body,
starting from the head up;
i feel the clouds separate and reform,
i feel dust particles dance away to other recitals.

only the sun discovers me now
appearing through the glass window pane
like
flash photography,
epileptic ecstasy,
blurred bokeh filters
fading in and out of focus;
like
strips of film being fed through the reel
and playing
feature length sunshine.

shannon ellis

curly headed lovers

curly headed lovers on a bus leaning upon each other,
cradled in amongst the masses.

at night their curls tangle around themselves -
they can no longer tell where each of their strands
end and begin;
they can no longer differentiate from themselves,
the bed creaks and echoes as they envelope
into each other at night.

the bus whirs and they edge closer
sharing yoghurt-coated biscuits
with a smile.
they are indistinguishable yet wholly different;
like one engine running on the same fuel
going opposite directions.

just like the wiry curls that sit upon their heads,
warping around the wheels and adjusting the driver's mirror;
they work in tandem, their laughs echo
amongst the metal and fabric,
until at last they rest their bodies side by side;
their laugh becoming quiet and the curls
unfurling into silence.

elements of an adored mind

the first hello

dear there is not a word for you-
but only descriptions.
you are all encompassing without knowing it,
you consume wholeheartedly with eyes screwed shut-

you are like
the bitterness of coffee as the first thing to touch my lips
in the dusky morning,
like the static electricity of old tapes locked away somewhere
but still quietly listened to in memories.

you are the interlude of each song,
the brief breath in between every phone call,

boy,

you are percussion and guitars plucked gently,
you are a call during a party;
a phone box seemingly forgotten.

you are my ripped jeans and ankle socks,
you are my dog-eared books and missing earphones,
you are the smell of old paper and my perfume,

but
boy,

you are yours, and you are only fragments of my mind now

but
boy,

i still anticipate the first hello.

shannon ellis

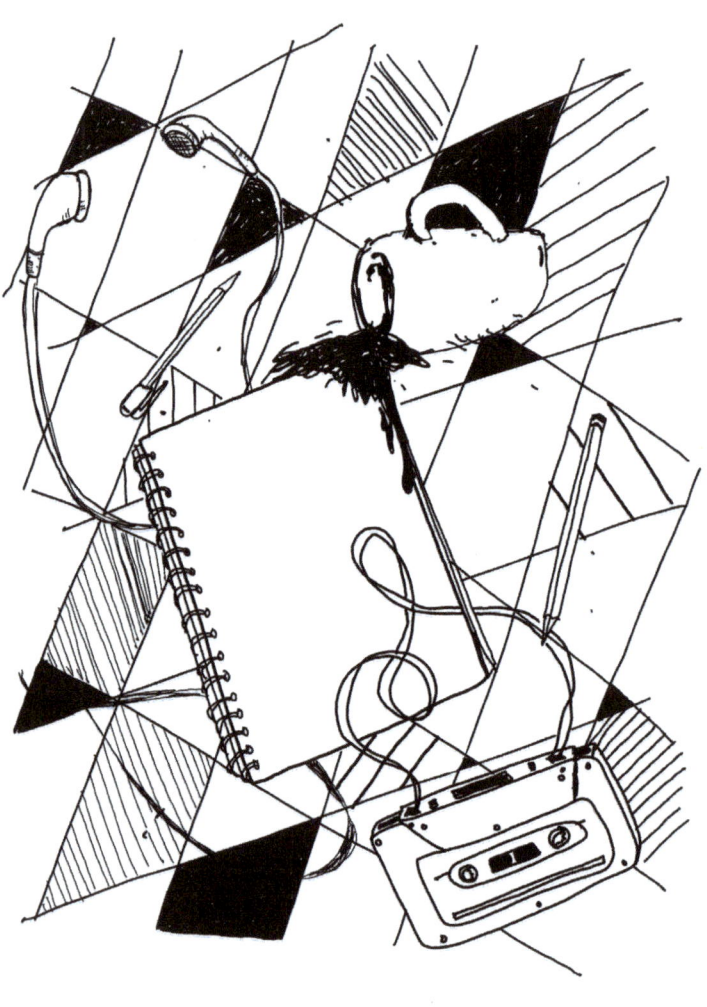

elements of an adored mind

quiet nights

i like quiet nights
like the ones you and i have,
when sitting is like an ethereal transition
from where we once were,
who we once were,
to who we are now.

a familiar face in a crowd of change,
a voice speaking in a tongue i recognise,
a body that has grown up beside mine
in tattered playgrounds and stuffy classrooms.

a girl that acts like a mirror to remind me
of time gone,
a recording of static laughter and cluttered spaces.
daisy chains and spiked sprite,
stark white tinged with orange -
of the sunsets we shared in the town of no-ones.

nonsense sprouted from intellect buried deep,
shared youth and fading stills of the lapses of judgement
and forgotten adventures.

i like quiet nights
like the ones you and i have.

shannon ellis

bare connections

take me somewhere that makes me a bare, breathing wonder;
somewhere that exists solely in your mind and in the gap
between our hands, preventing touch.

teach me the language of the untouched region that resides
in amongst your
synapses and sighs.

show me the landmarks that have stood the
test of time in your head,
your head that's been rattled around and colonised
too many times to count.

tell me the myths, the legends, the folklore
of your dusty memories
and invite me into your narrative.

elements of an adored mind

love

i talk about love as if i was in the room where she was born,
i talk about love as if i cradled her as a baby
and sang her lullabies,
i talk about love as if she lived beside me or along the hall -
i talk about love as if i walked with her every day to school
and pushed her bullies away.

i talk about love as if we stayed up watching movies
and eating popcorn on weekends.

i talk about love as if she's held my hand during struggle,
i talk about love like how the morning sounds,
i talk about love like how the rain smells.

i talk about love as if i've watched her
graduate and move away,
i talk about love as if i skype her
every second wednesday.

i talk about love like she stands by me daily-
i talk about love as if she reached into my chest
and took my heart
for safekeeping.

i talk about love like the idealistic body i am,
and she thanks me.

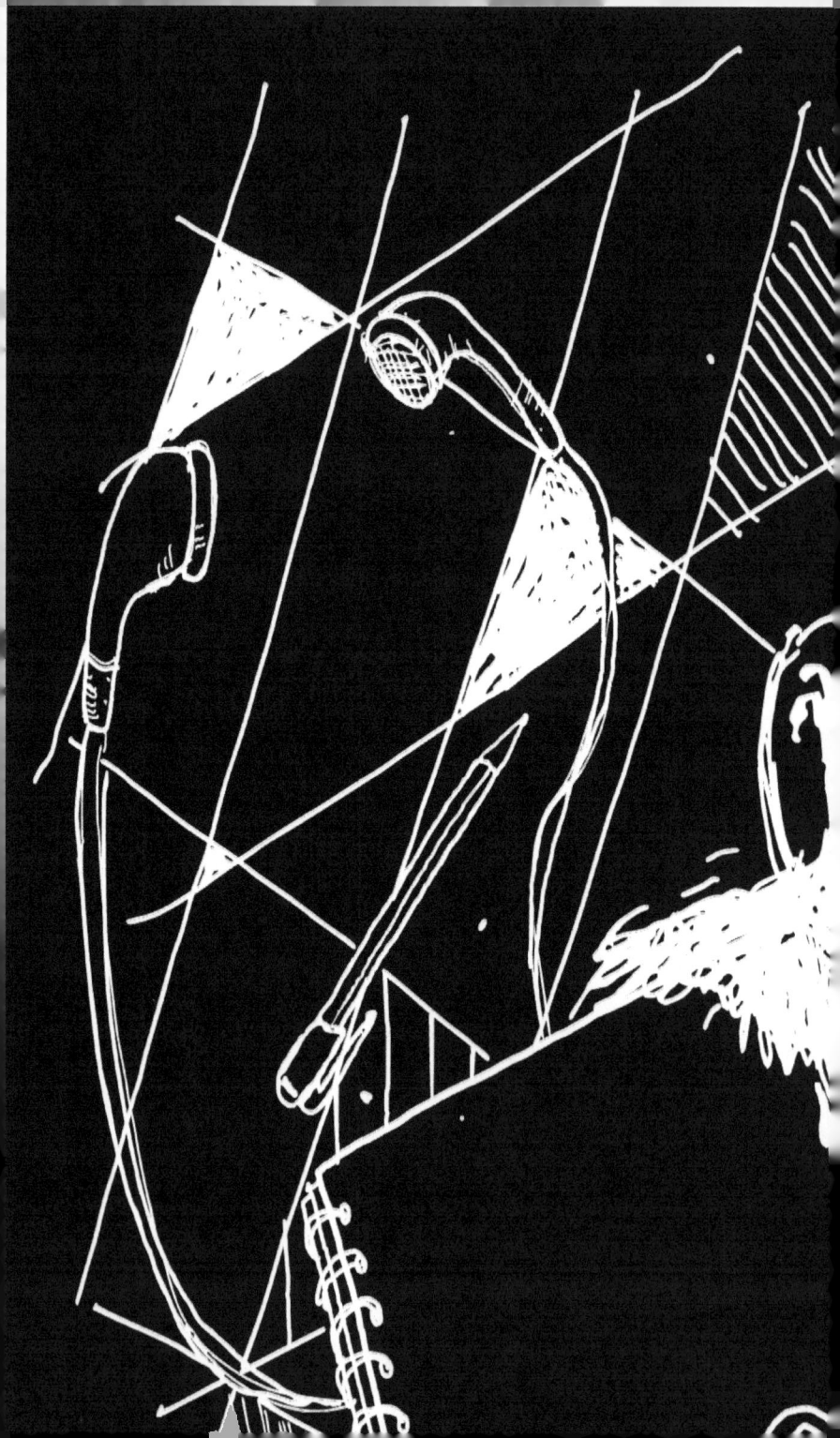

the wind

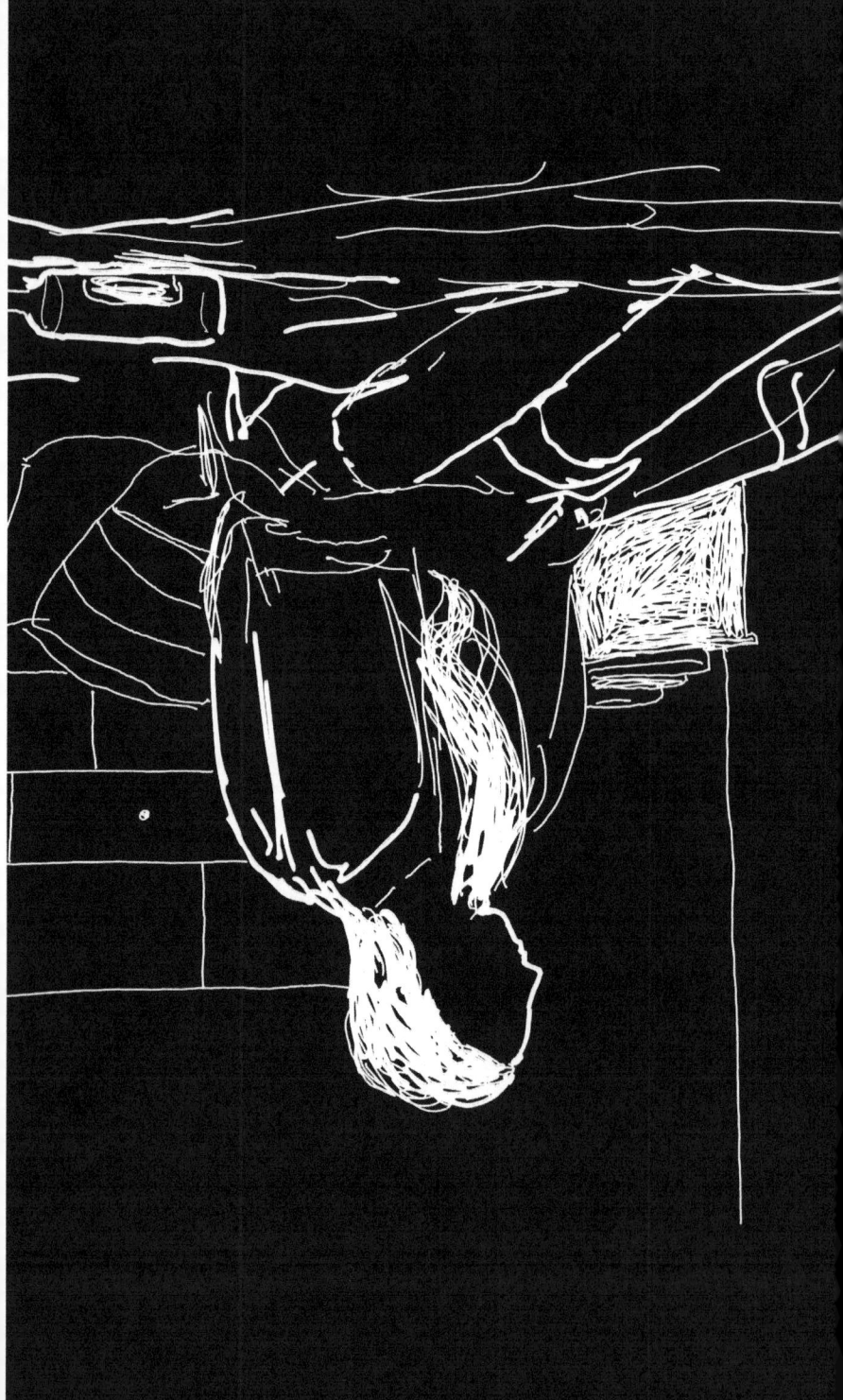

elements of an adored mind

quarantined

you quarantined me
into a room full of dust,
a dusty room with dusty air;
air that didn't work,
it made me cough, cough, cough.

into a room with bedsheets that smelled
of cheap wine and fake strawberry.

into a room with one window that revealed only
a brick wall painted blue-
the dust climbed up my nostrils,
it climbed up and up and up until
it latched onto my synapses and held tightly;
my eyes screwed shut,
the brick wall fell away, and I heard the bedsheets rustle.
the smell of that fermented fruit
disappeared.

suddenly i was seeing you quarantined;
in my mind you were there,
in a musty room with musty air;
air that didn't work;
it made you sneeze, sneeze, sneeze.

shannon ellis

elements of an adored mind

into a room with bedsheets that smelled
of acidic vodka and fake vanilla.

into a room with one window that only revealed
a wooden fence painted green-
the must invaded your senses,
it clung to your nose until
it reached your muddled brain and stayed there,
then your eyes fluttered shut
the fence became dismantled;
the bedsheets were replaced,
the acidic smell of clear spirit gone.

i saw you building a brick wall with blue paint prepared,
i watched you pour cheap wine over bedsheets
and smear fake strawberry into the fabric.

i saw you leave the room until it collected dust and then
i was brought here to watch it swirl.

shannon ellis

secrets

hidden behind locks of hair and glazed over stares,
hidden behind other words and loud noises,
hidden in the cloudy vision that follows her,
she knows these whispers like the back of her hand.

the warning sounds,
the hushes in the wind-
ears perked,
on alert.

she knows what those words mean
but it's a secret;
lips sealed.

hidden in the scarves she wears and lies she replies with,
hidden in the tattered makeup bag she carries;
hush,
it's a secret she can't disclose but now she's struggling
to find new hiding places.

her cupboard is too full,
and he always checks under the bed
her mouth is taped shut,
the sting of it reminds her to cover the imprints,
disguise the bluish hues,
make her voice small and delicate
and keep his dirty little secret.
hush,
it's a secret she can't disclose.

elements of an adored mind

make your eyes blind;
ears deaf,
mouth mute-
ignore the close stares,
the almost-caught gazes,
the exposed nearly's-
but not quite's.

shannon ellis

close encounters

i hold on to affection like a child does to their mother's leg;
tight and unrelenting.

you could skim my skin once and it would burn for decades,
you could gaze into my eyes for milliseconds
and i would immortalise
the moment in poetry and replay the hues
of your irises again and again.

words said in a rush whisper to me during the night
clearer than the first time i ever heard it.

you could crush my heart into a million fragments,
and i would instead think of that first encounter
where you complimented my smile.

i fall in love every day with another,
but hang onto the ones who came before like
old trinkets from childhood.

it paints scars onto my limbs, living like this,
giving everything to strangers expecting anything less
than the pain i receive.
but i keep scrapbooking laughs and collecting kisses
written at the ends of texts;
my body engulfs them whole without complaint,
and swallows up crooked-tooth grins and worn-out eyes
with ease.

elements of an adored mind

scents of a thousand strangers' perfumes linger in my hair,
refusing to leave;
coffee orders cling to my bed frame, surrounding me
in bitter, sweet blackened liquid.
i bathe in it
submerging myself fully into voices, faces, bodies
almost drowning in the masses.
i return with only the faint distance of close encounters.

shannon ellis

underground

tobacco burning lightly underneath the arches,
cigarettes were lit an emerging red, indoors-
clouds of smoke travel upwards to the bricked underground,
swaying, dancing, inhaling.

lights examining bodies in frenzy...
it was the dark night in a city suspended in time,
it was the dark night with light feet and
fruit-induced veins running wild.

elements of an adored mind

concrete

consisting, i remember,
closes full of scratched concrete-
that yellowing grey filter,
puddles not of rain
but of other things
in those enclosed flats.

cider
cigarettes
cold council- no heating
corridors smothered by a looming dog.

those green couches,
kitchens with no doors- clear view to the TV,
the garden looks far but the washing line asserts itself.

and those shakes running through that topsy turvy person;
that tenant revisited,
a friend by speech but not by feeling.

those flats held plasterboard with scorched sides,
cigarette butts flooded the carpets;
the curtains- doily lace.

i revisit those smoke screens -
these whispers of a place i shouldn't be in.

shannon ellis

dodgy conversations at a bus stop

a stranger with a family member's confidence,
a perception of closeness- unwarranted,
almost acting as if we'd met before.

spoke in start and stops,
erratic fever dream movements,
hazy disclaimers and uncomfortable statements
joined by the uncomfortable smell,
stance,
appearance,
mind state.

persevered;
heard my nervous laugh as an invitation
to his bedroom talk and
his life's prequel.

unhinged phrases and gazes,
ignored by the others-
my kindness snatched by him
and misplaced into his back-pocket.

that laughter,
a non-verbal plead for conclusion; a hope for allusion,
nevertheless, he heard it wrong and persisted with
his attitude and want for an imaginary something
clung to the wind rustling my hair.

the rumble of an engine finally sounding
as my prolonged rescue mission.

the clouds

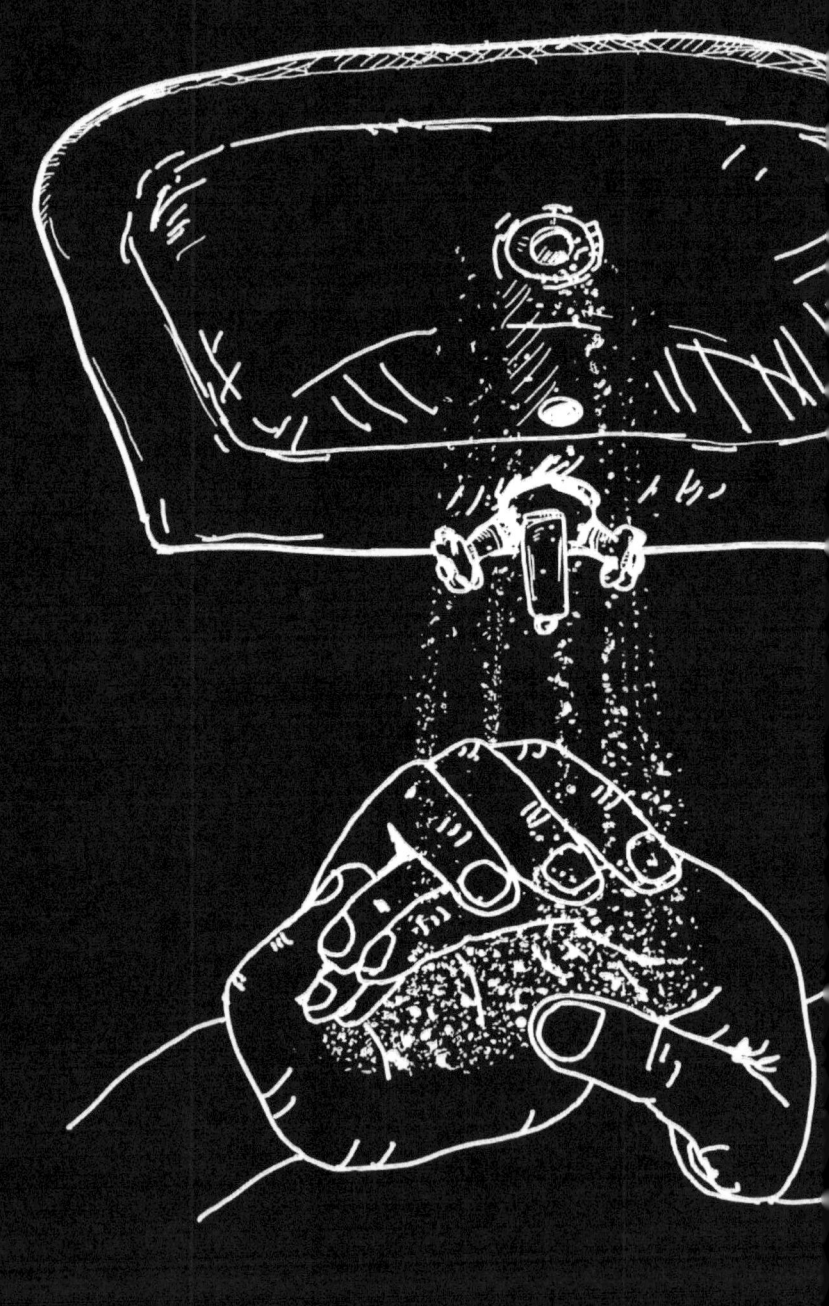

elements of an adored mind

the last summer

the last summer was video diaries and blurred snapshots.
full of paralysis and spine tingles that felt like
fancy wine you shouldn't touch.

nights were lilac and navy,
bonfire smoke mixed with fizzy overspills
of boundaries on sand.
imprints of hands, bodies, lips
lingered on those sunrises, and laughter
was spelled out in the sunset.

between them grew daisy chains and picnic blankets.
the heady smell of smoke
and mowed lawns;
confused pass-outs until
the morning braced us again and the heat grew stronger,
with each intake of breath.

fruit was sweeter in the last summer;
fireworks erupted in skies and stomachs.

slowly though, the coldness crept in;
the garden began biting against our caress
and we left it all behind-
not knowing
how much we'd miss the ashes and the cigarette stubs.

the last summer came and went
like blowing a kiss into the air,
it has faded into pale yellow
like a beloved polaroid in father's leather wallets
caressing the better times.

shannon ellis

readjustment

a draught tickles at my neck tonight and it feels like
your coldness;
only sweeter, deeper somehow
without your snarl embedding my home.

the natural breeze etches the yelling immortalised
into my bedroom walls.
your favourite tea mug continues to greet me with distaste -
with your snarls -
and that same draught
knocks it from its shelf.
suddenly
i forget your name.

elements of an adored mind

bittersweet

i am drained of the peach iced tea sweetness
you fed me
in the unrelenting heat of our
fairy light insides.

you said the sugar spoiled me
and all i could see were the heart cavities
inside the mouth you corroded.

the bees keep blowing up my phone,
they want to know where i've been.
business was good until i left and
went sugar-free
no iced tea,
no you and me.

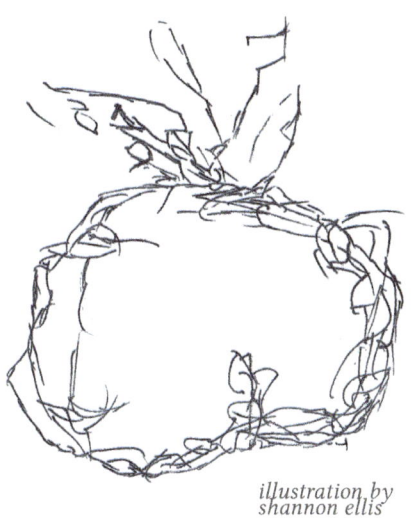

*illustration by
shannon ellis*

shannon ellis

gold dust

tainted gold dust trickles down my drain
as your fingerprints leave me.

the glistening rocks i reserved for you
crumbled into dirt once you left, the door remained open;
mercury tears flooding through our threshold
in hurried measure.

elements of an adored mind

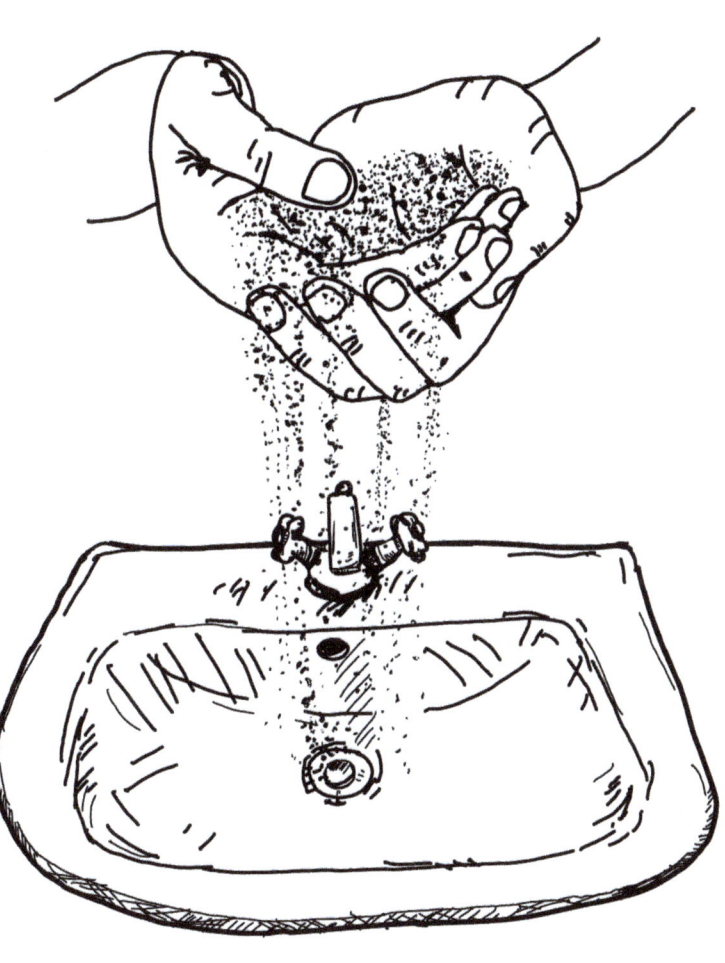

shannon ellis

cherry wine

our lungs soaked in cherry wine that night;
the bottle empty, like your words.

i knew it was over when the cigarette ash
fell to the carpet,
i knew it was over when the soft hum
of our record player ceased
and you replaced the sound with half-hearted
murmur.

the slight intoxication swirled
in my aching stomach as you stood up unsteadily,
leaving citrus and silence lingering
behind your steps.

that bottle still sits there now, empty,
and your voice remains in the neck of it;
as a reminder of the bitterness.

elements of an adored mind

embers

you used to run sparkles down my spine:
the embers would always cling to our bedsheets
as you moved the fire along until
it burned out leaving charcoal dust embedded
in my skin
spelling out our truths.

shannon ellis

sipping tea

your cigarettes and tea-stained shirts,
your chapped lips and coffee-coloured eyes,
your scratchy voice and soft vinyl records.

it was a disaster from the start, one i fell fully into
willingly, blissfully.

i tripped into the vortex of you and i didn't care about the
scratches i got,
all i cared about was you, my natural disaster;
a storm that rocked the boat,
a hurricane that shook my heart,
and a tsunami that drowned me.

i didn't care about her and i didn't care she was here
before me,
all i cared about were the innocent nights
spent sipping tea with you.
i didn't care that i compared you to the stars
when you were simply human.

i didn't care that you never saw me the same way and
i didn't care that it took a while until you did.
i didn't care that you changed as time went on,
i was still comparing you to the stars even in the daytime.
i didn't care that you were staying out later
because afterwards you would still come back to me
and sip tea.

and i didn't care that i smelt another's perfume,
i didn't care that i was left alone all day and
i didn't care that you never tried to hide it.
i still didn't care when you started drinking whisky
instead of tea with me.

elements of an adored mind

i didn't care that you said her name sometimes
instead of mine
and i didn't care that you forgot i was still here
loving you.

i didn't care that you swapped the teacup for a bottle
because when the bottle wore off you were the same person
i met at the beginning.

and i didn't care that you started smoking more
and speaking less
and that you were drifting away
because i knew you knew
i'd always be here to sip tea with.

and i didn't care when your words became different
from the mesmerising ones i had heard before
and that this meant it was almost the end.

i didn't care that i was left to look after you
when she broke your heart
and i didn't care that you stopped looking me in the eye,
i didn't care that you had fallen in love with her,
because when she broke your heart you started sipping tea
with me again.

and i didn't care that you had stopped loving me
and i didn't care that you wanted me gone
and i didn't care that you told me to leave
because at night we'd still sip tea.

shannon ellis

and i didn't care that when i woke up the next day
you were gone
because i knew you'd be back for me.
and i didn't care that you never came back for tea
and i didn't care that you had left me.

and i did care when i realised i was alone now,
and suddenly the tea i drank before didn't taste as sweet
and i did care when you came back late one night,
your eyes bloodshot and watery.

and i really didn't care when i closed the door on you,
knowing you didn't really show up for me
i said goodbye to your
cigarettes and tea-stained shirts,
your chapped lips and coffee-coloured eyes,
your scratchy voice and soft vinyl records.

the rain

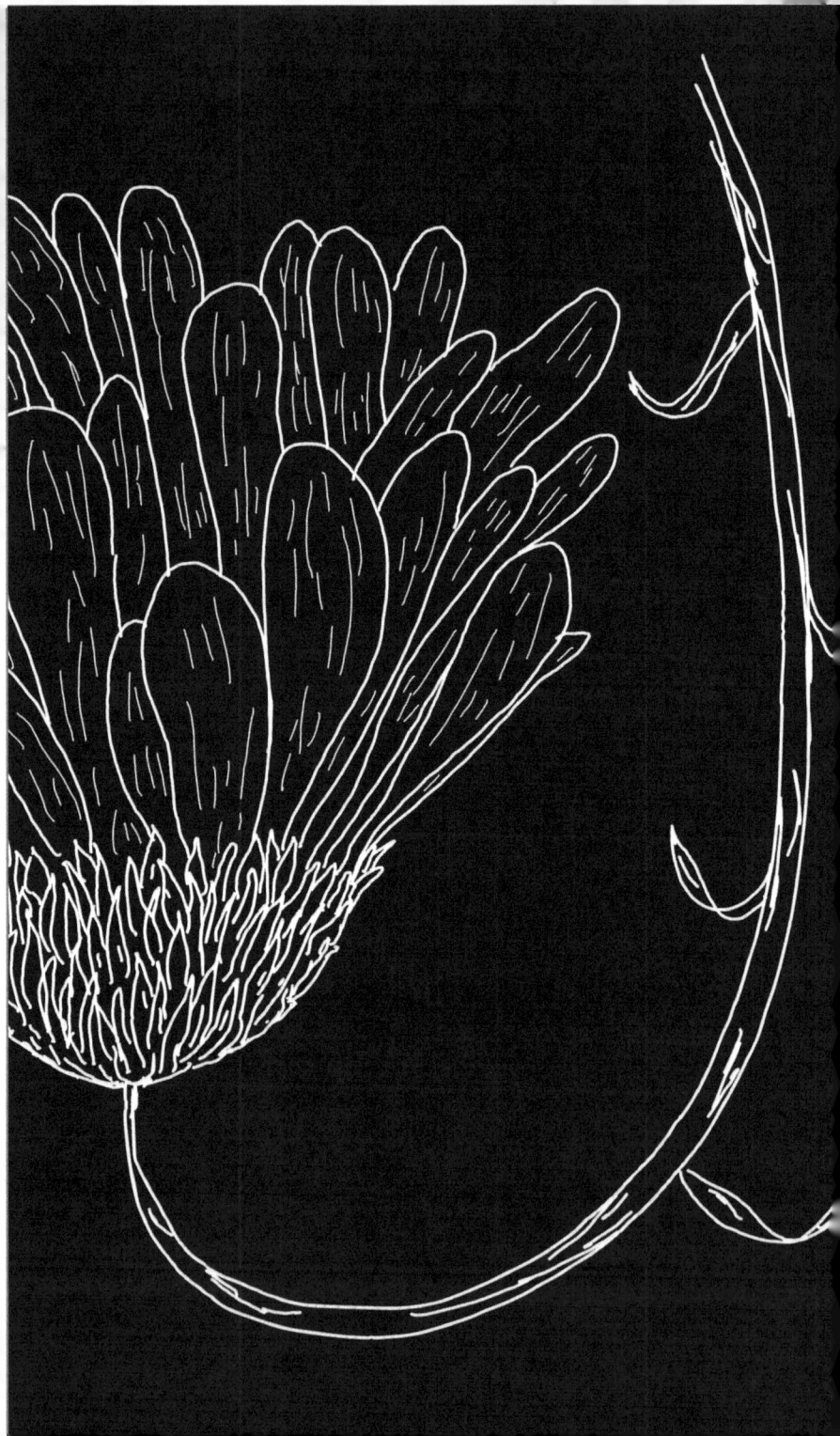

elements of an adored mind

daisy plucker

i often ask myself who chose the daisy
to become the flower continuously
heartbroken and torn to pieces;
you never see a hand pluck the petals of a rose,
asking it to be loved.

is it because the rose would make you bleed?
with its thorns reminding you of love's
pain.

is it the red that stains its silk,
telling you your fragile heart is the same colour?
why is the daisy allowed to burn in our selfish grasp?
why does the whiteness of their petals trigger no fear
of the questions we ask it while ripping its delicate limbs
from its body?

i wonder if the daisy asks us the questions back,
or does it instead whimper and seek out
the roses,
the sunflowers,
the dandelions,
to relieve them from the searing hotness of heartbreak.

why does a daisy's petal feel like
wishes unwished in our palms?
why does the yellow of its centre look
more appealing when laid bare?
why do we ask the daintiest flower
if they love us or love us not?

shannon ellis

i think it's because we couldn't handle
the harshness of a rose
to fragment our bones and slit our hearts;
the daisy delivers us a softer blow,
we can look at it and smile with the result of rejection.

but with a rose we sit and drown in the blood
running down our fragile fingers
from the thorns that tried to warn us.

elements of an adored mind

distance

i've been floating around you for a while now,
i'm orbiting you and this gravity
won't let up.

but you've been distant:
you're trying to shake me off,
get rid,
eradicate.

this love tinged with dust,
it's getting old now but
it's all i know.

there's nothing stopping you from dropping
me and yet,
you keep me dangling at arm's length,
but i'm still in your
blue view.

you say words now exhausted from meaning,
our wires are crossed;
connected,
woven,
and i can't find any pliers to cut me from us.

i feel the bed shift at night,
but it's cold -
as if you've taken all the covers.

shannon ellis

the truth is, i don't feel the dent of your form
in the mattress anymore.
the only indication of you beside me are shallow breaths;
my mind has been tossed into the star-stained sky,
your gaze has shifted in the dark.
where are you?
why has this distance entered our space?

elements of an adored mind

podcast

a podcast put me to sleep in your arms and
awoke you to the unresolved feelings
lingering somewhere,
with someone
in another bed.

shannon ellis

remnants

the acquaintance of a stranger's lover bounds over
and tells me your life story.
she tells it in a voice
carved out of closeness and
first-hand touch.

your hearts once entwined like
a field of dying flowers, yet
the scent stays permitted
on her collarbone.

your fingertips glisten within
her lip gloss top coat,
i see the specks of your gaze in
her gaze, and she laughs nervously
as i recognise your old mannerisms in
her hands.

i look at her and she sees your hands on my waist,
the silk of our bedsheets,
and the fog of our shower screen.

she shrinks into the wine glass that she grasps and
i look again, seeing
the tattered boxes and broken
cries of her ending with you.

and i wonder if one day
you will ever become reflections
in my eyes looking at the one
who came after.

elements of an adored mind

shannon ellis

acquainted strangers

strangers know the best of me.
they get my biggest smiles,
they hear my best jokes;
the sad irony stares -
that the ones living next door to my heart
see the worst version of myself.

no, my kindest hours aren't reserved for you;
my longest lover, my birth mother,
and my closest others.

instead they get my tired eyes,
frustrated sighs,
they get shattered cries,
my outbursts,
my lies.

elements of an adored mind

heart

my heart is like an oil spill splayed
across a pavement,
it reflects into itself and offers up rainbow technicolour
in a world of muted grey.

my heart stops people in the street,
my heart is like an oil spill clinging
onto the soles of your shoes
refusing to let go.

all the while
you remain unaware of the reality,
that your footfall stampeded
into my puddled mess of a psychedelic heart,
leaving the rest of my body with a hole;
a rippled, ricocheted gap.

the oil spill slowly dispersing down the gutter,
into the dull blackness of everything
instead of that initial glistening illusion
my heart was before
you.

shannon ellis

exhibition

step into the desert with me and
jump through the ocean;
watch as you float on inflated egos,
watch as you kick up a fuss in the sand,
watch as it retaliates.

climb your mountains
while i fill in the gaps you left,
finding footing.

breathe as if you use my lungs
on a short-term loan
which claims interest.

shannon ellis

passive transport mind strings

when making journeys void of distraction
i jump into the deepest recesses of my mind.
i leave longings of different outcomes
in lay-bys;
i transfer scar tissue onto the golden leaves,
the pavement takes a hit, maybe two,
from familiar fists and cries.

lampposts receive kisses from sloppy dream memories,
that have faded into a veiny duck-egg blue.
hedges call me by nickname;
and it's something that only happens when
walking alone,
driving alone,
commuting alone.

the air pinches my nose with the excessive salt
you poured on dinners already salted,
the wind smells like
cheap beer and cigarette smoke without a hint
of a pub nearby.

and i realise you follow me,
in the quiet moments,
the in-betweens,
clinging onto my jacket like
a jagged thorn unwilling to let go until
another voice cuts into my brainwaves.

the surroundings return to what they are,
no reminders present in my peripheral vision;
only whispers of a figure somewhere still unknown,
crossing the road to the intersections i avoid.

the thunder storm

elements of an adored mind

trigger run

continuously running from warrants and wrongdoings but
when i share your name, it ends up being me
shackled,
handcuffed,
punished by guilt, rattling with anxiety.

paternally absent -
your footsteps mirror mine but i'm stepping into yours
the wrong way
and you keep swerving me.
i bet the sound of sirens acts as a quiet lullaby
haunting your eardrums.

the sound of wind chimes and birds are foreign to you -
they can't awake your mind,
only the smell of corrupt hideouts
and reoccurring mistakes.

the recipe for disaster was passed down from you to me
but i can't cook it the same way,
i'm missing ingredients and the penmanship has faded
on the crumpled paper with this shared damage,
i can't win this trigger run.

shannon ellis

father

your tattooed arms tattooed bruises onto her skin-
i never saw;
your tainted breath hushed insults like
a religious prayer in the morning.
you swallowed poison as if it could
save your diminishing life.

your lips never uttered sorry and your eyes were always
simmering, angry, underneath.
i couldn't hate you despite the sickness that clung
to my throat every time you exploded;
yet, i still feel the underlying fear that encased my bones
when they were crushed by a hug.

because i saw the candlestick that wouldn't burn
but bruise,
i felt the plate skid across the floor
and into my knee,
i felt the shaky breath of my mother
when she tried to say goodnight
without shedding a tear.

i saw the looks you avoided and the taunts you initiated,
you are ill, i know,
but you still haunt me like the bitter smell of vomit;
as if you've coughed your sickness up into my veins and now
my blood is contaminated with it.

but i forget you are my blood.
your tendencies to torture unknowingly
warps my brain into an amnesia i can't escape from;
i can't remember a time where i was a daddy's girl without
feeling the bruising of my mother and the sickness of your
sickness.

elements of an adored mind

i can't remember you being a gentle father without
my nostrils being filled with the sour scent of
alcohol and cloudy smoke.

i keep you in the rotting parts of my environment like
broken relationships and disappearing play parks.
you are slowly becoming a fragment of my memories,
a stranger i once vaguely knew.

but i never knew you and your
explanations and acclamations
of sobriety won't change that.
i know you mean well but your attempts are ill;
all you do is take up brain space
and make my childhood feel like
a festering wound.

most memories i pick are negative and i know it's unfair but
the weight is unbalanced when it comes to happy places
and words, and the ones that exist are much too rare
they become engorged by the bitter tragedy
of your broken frame.

i love you, deep down it is impossible not to,
but you are toxic, you leech into my
mind when i don't want to fall
into the darkness you gave,
so i love you, really i do
but i just can't find it in myself to like you.

shannon ellis

soap

i clean my mouth out with your soap,
after making my own and you replying with
darling, don't use that, mine is better, you know that.
but you said darling like a curse,
like poison spilling from your lips,
like blood in words.

once i used a different shampoo and you said
do you not appreciate what i give to you?
this is what i have chosen for you, if you love me
you'll use it.
but your shampoo wasn't good: it was weak and cheap,
it didn't make my dandruff or the itch on my scalp disappear,
all it did was exude your darlings of danger and
if-you-love-me's.

i want my own soap.
i want to choose it at the store.
i want it to stand on its own in the shower;
i don't want your soap but
you say if i don't use yours i will have
nothing.

yesterday, i chose another perfume,
and the smell of violence was released when you found out;
i may not want your soap or shampoo or your perfume,
or even maybe, possibly, you but
at least the makeup you buy me works
to retain the sweet scent that surrounds you.

elements of an adored mind

manner

i'm someone's heartbreak,
i'm someone's healing manner,
i'm someone's vulgar vault of vices,
i'm someone's peach smile and hazy terracotta memories
hidden in wooden chests.

i'm someone's needle on a record,
i'm someone's addiction and someone's
withdrawal symptoms -
clinging to their veins,
aching in their bones,
cloudy in their eyes.

shannon ellis

elements of an adored mind

harsh

your words are carved from
abandoned infants' tears and
an innocent man's handcuffs;
how harsh you are,
how it sears my lips
receiving yours.

the rainbow

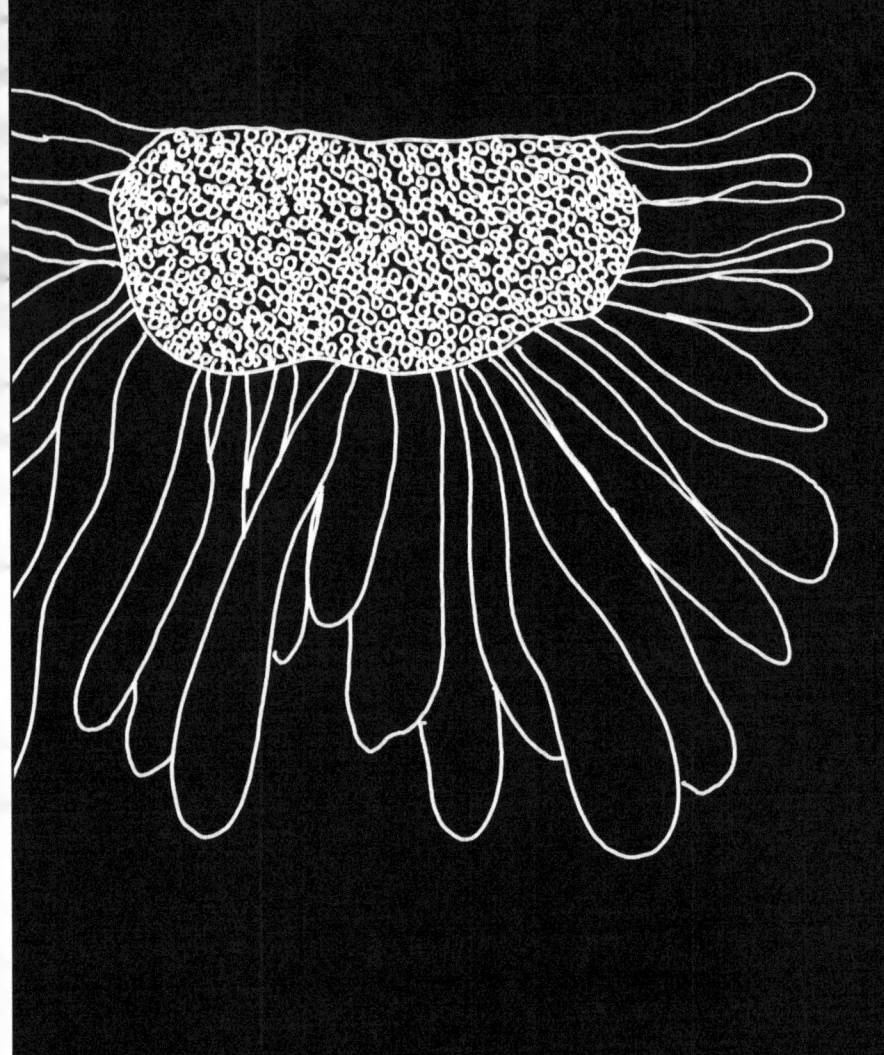

elements of an adored mind

familiar

you're so familiar,
like another limb;
even though you're out of reach now,
i always feel you beside
me.

like the sister i never had,
waves separate us, but
we're on the same wavelength.
i miss the little parts like
failed cakes and TV breaks.

best friend,
here's your muse piece.

shannon ellis

ode to my bedsheets

this is an ode to my bedsheets;
the ones that captured the bad dreams and
keep my tear-stained pillows safe.

the ones that hold my blood stains in their palms
with gentle adoration
and collect my hair strands;
they record my yawning sighs and
create endless loops on an EP track.

my bedsheets,
the ones that tangle and twist alongside my restlessness,
they whisper comforts to me
in the dark night-time moments.
pull me closer and i'll recite the lullabies
they taught me in-between
sleep-drunk seconds.

elements of an adored mind

buttons

i'd rather unbutton your mind than your shirt,
unzip your lips, wait for your brain to fall out and
spill all over me,
instead of the jeans you wear and what's underneath.
i'd rather kiss your thoughts that pour from ears tainted red.
i'd drink them in as they leak from your human pores.
i'd rather steal your eyes than your breath and rather catch
you breathless because of my brain
being tangled with yours;
not my legs.

rather revel in the redemption of our words and take a seat
in your psyche
instead of one in your bed.
i'd take my time piecing you together,
only to dismantle you over again,
and slowly run my fingertips past your whispered outcries.

i'd rather feel the beating of a heart inside you
telling me there's human
beside me,
i'd rather touch your very soul that shakes for me
more than anything else you possess,
i'd cradle it in my arms while you watch,
with broken - fixed - eyes.

there are places i'd like to see of you,
but none lie underneath a belt;
your being,
your reaching complexity is all i want to observe,
with eyes, my eyes, so
fixated,
fascinated,
enamoured
with you.

shannon ellis

acquired astrology

i met him in a planetarium;
he was staring at me and not the glaring rocks above,
and my heart leapt into orion.

the dome smiled as the sky rotated.
constellations clapped when you touched me,
and the stars descended into your irises like
diamond-encrusted shards of tape
recording the first time you orbited me.

elements of an adored mind

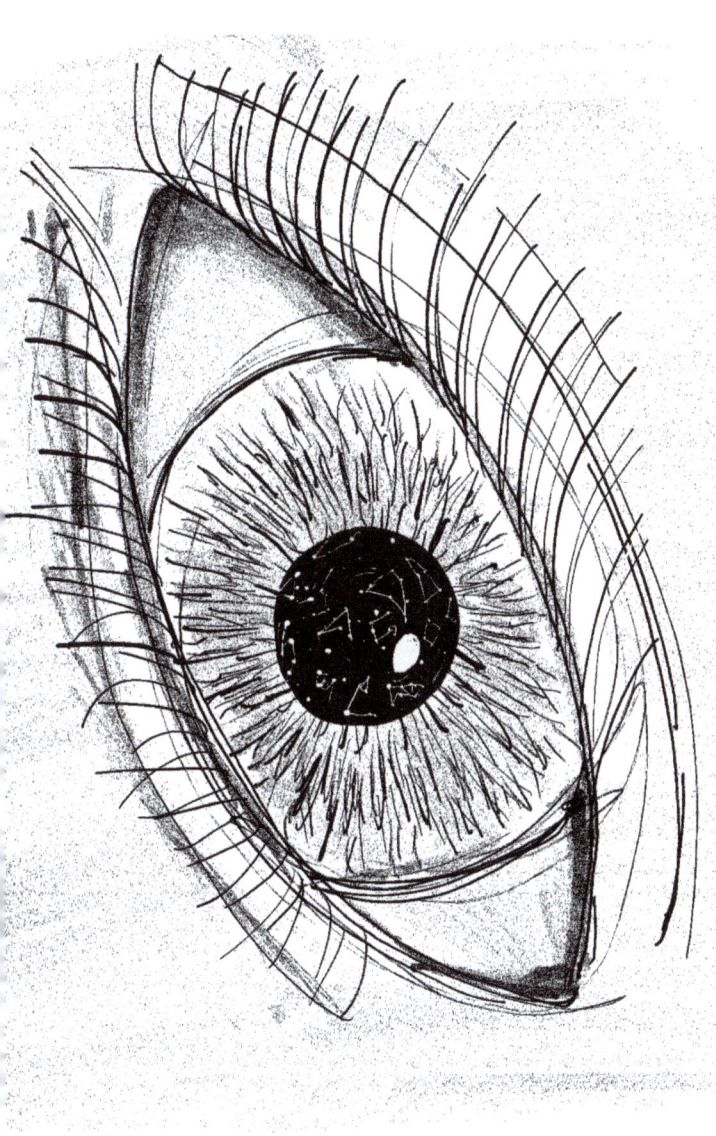

shannon ellis

chords

there are chords
i think birthed you;
i hear them and there you are.

elements of an adored mind

fault lines

sometimes i look at your hands and
watch clouds form in the fault lines that etch your skin,
and sometimes i look at the clouds and see your eyes
in the white, untouchable wisps.

you are the objects that surround me,
the air i gasp for,
the water i dive deep into.

your reflection remains embedded
in every raindrop that falls,
you've changed me from someone always begging for sun
to someone who longs for the hazy downpour
just so i can catch your gaze in the clear watery puddles
below me.

and then you ask why i stare at you for so long,
and i cannot answer.
so, next time you see me lingering,
know it's because the trees told me
your favourite colour last night,
and the flowers tickled at my feet
as if they were your fingertips;
know that the yellow of the sun
is the same exact shade you make me feel,
and that my music interludes at the sound of your voice.

know that my hunger pangs
begin in my heartstrings and travel
to my toes when you say my name;
know that the only birdsong i've ever heard is your laugh,
and the thunder in a storm mimics your tired sighs.

shannon ellis

i couldn't escape you even if i wanted to.
your existence has morphed into my smile lines and freckles;
i couldn't look at my own face without seeing yours,
and that's the only kind of re-occurring reminder i look
forward to.

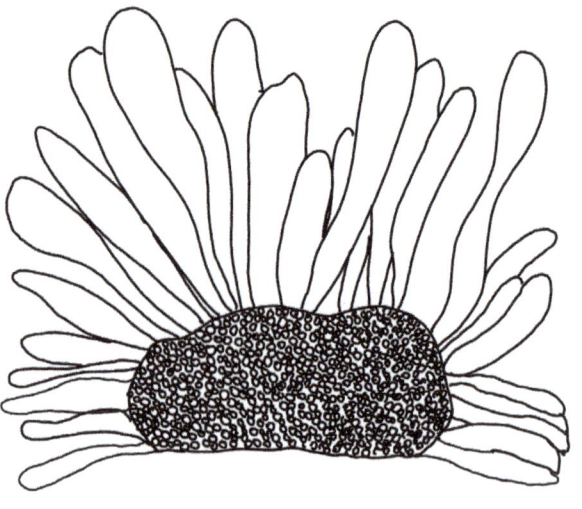

elements of an adored mind

your daughter

if bee stings felt sweet on our skin
we wouldn't resent them,
and if i knew you better it wouldn't swell so.

now i'm trying; instead of seeing your arm's past actions
i see the art displayed on them
and appreciate the beauty you wanted crafted.
when i hear your voice i will try not to think of its tone
when it was raised,
i'm looking past the fear and seeing the fragility
of you.

you're more human than what i used to accept,
and our blood is the same shade;
it's only fair we try again because it doesn't fade
like the struggling memories of you have.

i think it's finally sunk in deep to your war scars,
that the clock still ticks even if you're not looking,
that life can and will go on without you if you let it.

so now where i used to see resentment, father;
i can see resolution in you.

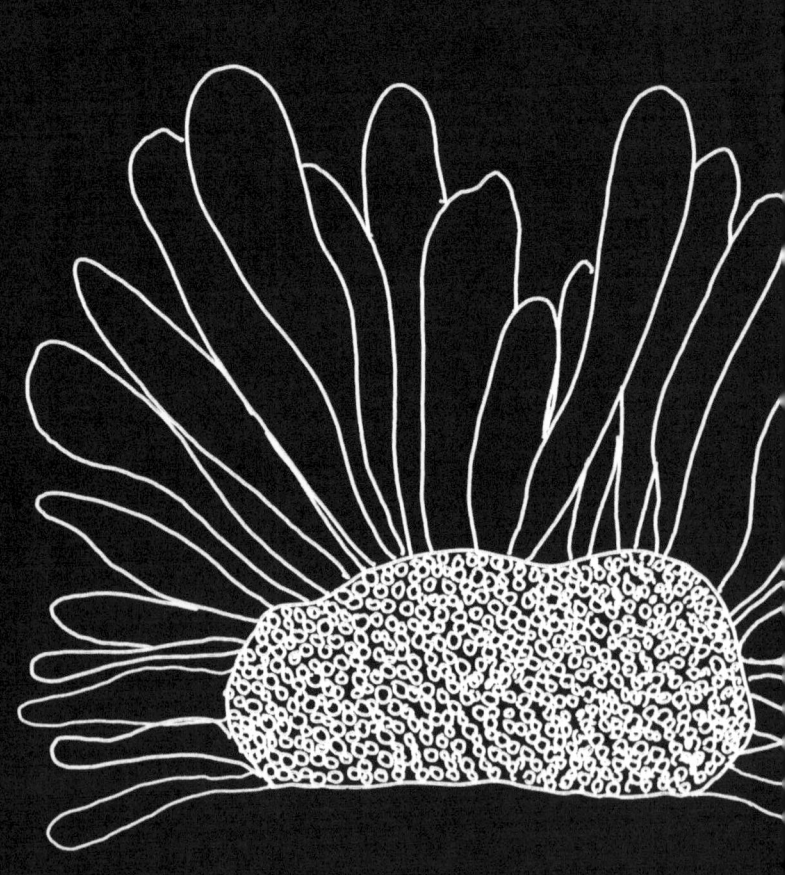

about the poet

Shannon Ellis is a poet from Scotland. She is studying English literature at university and writes short stories on occasion. She focuses on writing about personal experience centering around love, loss, relationships, forgiveness and tackling mental health issues and trauma. She usually ties these themes in with her love of nature and metaphor. Her hope is that her work can resonate with anyone experiencing similar issues that her poetry reflects upon, bringing solace and peace to others. Shannon can be found on instagram as @sipping_tea_poetry.

about the illustrator

Ruben Ramires is an artist from Portugal, who lives in Houston, USA. He is a poet, illustrator, and actor who uses raw lines and humour to talk about autobiographical, sensitive, and everyday topics. He hopes that his honesty will demistify mental health, poetry, and art in general. Ruben can be found on Instagram as @RubenRamires.

praise for *elements of an adored mind*

"'only the sun discovers me now'- what a perfect scene setter. From the moment I picked up 'Elements of an Adored Mind' I was hooked. Split into 6 chapters, this collection takes the reader on a journey through love lost and found, heartbreak and sorrow, and finally, acceptance and the joys that can be found in forgiving. It openly explores feelings and emotions relating to complicated relationships and raw, relatable sentiments. For anyone needing to hear words of reassurance this is a stunning, unputdownable read. A powerful collection of thought provoking poetry and prose from a talented and promising debut author."
- Gemma Marie, author of *The Anatomy of Wanting*

"This book of poetry exemplifies all the highs and lows of falling in love: the beautiful melodic beginning, and the harsh, bitter end. Shannon takes us through every step of falling in love, writing with such ease and poignance that we are there with her, holding onto her words the way "a child does their mother's leg; tight and unrelenting." *elements of an adored mind* is a gorgeous journey. It's a perfect book for those who have ever felt the complicated, beautiful, tangled voyage that is love."
- Hinnah Mian, author of *To Build a Home*

"*Elements of an Adored Mind* is both a bold confession and gentle reassurance in poetry form. In this elegant collection, Shannon speaks to a lover, to figures from the past, to the reader, and most poignantly, to herself in carefully painted stories and memories. Her words are thoughtful, meaningful, and proud of the enduring feminine spirit that soars on each page. Shannon is a powerful voice in poetry that should not be missed."
- Faren Rajkumar, author of *Paper Flowers*

www.ingramcontent.com/pod-product-compliance
Lightning Source LLC
Chambersburg PA
CBHW061211070526
44583CB00025B/3205